Scattered Glimpses

Scattered Glimpses

LEAVES OF POETRY
by
Paul Ray

Sonray Press
publisher

*The passage of scripture used in the
Preface of this book (Matthew 24:35)
is from the New International Version
New Testament published by the Zondervan
Corporation, Copyright 1973 by New York
Bible Society International.*

*The quotation used in the
Prologue of this book was written by
Clive Staples Lewis (1898-1963)
from his book "Reflections On The Psalms"
chapter 1, page 5, paragraph 8.*

Copyright 2009 by Paul Ray

All rights reserved.
No part of this book may be reproduced or transmitted in any form or by any means, electronic or mechanical, including photocopying, recording, or by any information storage and retrieval system, without written permission from the publisher.

For information, contact:
Sonray Press, 1320 Cedar Lane, Charlotte, NC 28226

Printed In the United States of America
Sonray Press First Edition

Cover and layout format by gary hixson

ISBN 978-0-578-03646-5

Dedicated to
Patty, my angel
Alex, my eagle
and Maggie, my little busy bee.
*Thank you for all of your
love and support.*

Table of Contents

1	Preface
2	Prologue
5	Because He Thought Of You
6	Writing Love Notes
7	It's Time To Get Up
8	Come Back Home My Son
10	Car Problems
12	The Land Of Pleasant Dreams
14	What My Bible Means To Me
15	Cleaning The Bathroom
16	Ring The Bell
18	My Kind Sweet Sister
19	The Spot
21	Be Steadfast
22	Remember Christ
23	Whatever You Do To Haiti
25	Thank You For The Christmas Lights
26	New Home Welcome
27	Compared To God
28	When A Child Leaves Home
29	The Dog Head Cookies
31	One Special Night
32	Please Give Me A Pen
33	At The Trumpet Call

[TABLE OF CONTENTS]

35	Hello and Goodbye
36	A Headache
37	Through The Twilight
38	It's Not Because
39	Don't Let Pride Get In The Way
41	It's God Who Sees Everything
42	Some Good Questions
43	Why You Are So Beautiful
44	These Twenty Seven Years
45	If Jesus Came Back Here Tonight
46	The Sweet Lullaby
47	I'm Proud Of You Son
48	The Fall Of The Mighty Kong
49	My Mother's Love
51	A Message By The Sea
52	Turn The Radio Off!
53	For All You Do For Scouts
54	What Is My Purpose Here?
55	The Time I Spend
56	A Christian Prayer
57	Fireworks With The Family
58	From Pieces Of Wood
59	A Lifeless Heart
60	Symphonic Ecstasy
61	When I See You
62	House Church With The Hixsons

Preface

     One of the most beautiful and intriguing things about poetry is that it touches and reaches each person differently. It is similar to the Bible (which is also full of poetic verse) in that you can read the same verse or passage over and over for a long period of time and something new will jump out at you each time you read it. It is always new and refreshing like today's morning newspaper, and it never goes out of style, since truth will always remain true to the end of time.
     I think a lot of this has to do with the experiences that each of us has gone through and continues to go through each day of our lives. Each time we read a familiar passage of scripture or familiar poem, we tie into it new experiences and emotions from our lives which speak to each of us differently every day. Poetry is like a "connection of the dots" to our lives, with each of us making a new and different connection every time we read it.

Paul Ray

"Heaven and earth will pass away, but my words will never pass away."
     JESUS IN MATTHEW 24:35

Prologue

It seems to me appropriate, almost inevitable, that when that great Imagination which in the beginning, for Its own delight and for the delight of men and angels and (in their proper mode) of beasts, had invented and formed the whole world of Nature, submitted to express Itself in human speech, that speech should sometimes be poetry. For poetry too is a little incarnation, giving body to what had been before invisible and inaudible.

FROM "REFLECTIONS ON THE PSALMS"
BY C.S. LEWIS

Scattered Glimpses

Because He Thought Of You

When God walked on the earth one day
He saw a lovely sight
The hills rolled on with shades of green
With lakes that glistened bright
The trees were splendid in their form
The sky was big and blue
But then God stopped and smiled awhile
Because He thought of you.

The waterfalls were beautiful
To watch as He walked by
And as He did a rainbow formed
That sprang up in the sky
He smelled the scent of flowers there
In fields of grass they grew
And then God beamed a long long time
Because He thought of you.

The birds sang different melodies
To make His heart feel glad
The moose and elk walked up to Him
And knew He was their dad
The beaver and the chipmunk came
And chattered with Him too
But then God grinned from ear to ear
Because He thought of you.

Then God brought evening to the earth
And let His sunset spread
He brought the stars to twinkle on
While nature went to bed
Then one more time He looked at all
The things He made and knew
And then God laughed with joy all night
Because He thought of you.

Writing Love Notes

It's good to send a thoughtful card and always a good start
Especially when that card has words that come right from the heart;
What joy it is to get the mail and see a note of love
It brightens up a person's day to know they've been thought of.

So many times we're caught up with the trials that come our way
And fail to take a moment to encourage every day;
It only takes a word of love to turn a life around
So plant the seeds and watch God make the miracles abound.

Handwritten notes it's sad to say have fallen in decline
But still sometimes a spark of hope comes through a Valentine;
The greatest way to show our love of course is through our deeds
But taking time to write love notes meet everybody's needs.

So get your pen and paper out and start to write today
And share God's love with someone else to brighten up their day;
Don't let a day of yours go by without a note or two
Be sent to someone needing love 'cause that's the thing to do.

It's Time To Get Up

It's time to get up
To shine and to share
Jump out of yourself
And show that you care.

Groom out the grumbles
Rejoice and be glad
Give all the praise to
Your heavenly Dad.

Splash Christ on your face
Brush faith in your hair
Jump deep into joy
And know God is there.

The whistle has blown
To start a new day
So wake up and walk up
To what comes your way.

The love of the Lord
Is the life that you live
So get up and give up
What God gave to give.

Come Back Home My Son

A little boy had run away -
Who ran from hurt at home
His sack contained a sleeping bag,
A teddy bear and comb.

The truth was out - he made a mess
By telling of a lie
He blamed the innocent of wrong
Which made his father cry.

The little boy felt awful for
The thing that he had done
But just as he came home again
Some words caused him to run.

He overheard his father say
While standing by the door,
"He broke my heart so bad that I
Can't stand it anymore."

At that the boy packed up his things
And left without a note
But soon his dad did call for him
With sadness in his throat.

"I hurt for you and long for you
I know what you have done -
I will forgive your every sin
Please come back home my son!"

The little boy ran in the woods
And with some limbs and leaves
He made a tent and crawled inside
And burrowed under these.

[COME BACK HOME MY SON]

He cried out loud for a long time
"Dad please forgive my sin.
I hurt someone and hurt you too
And should not be your kin."

It came to pass the boy did hear
His father calling out
A pleading cry to come on home
Which caused the boy to shout.

At that the dad ran to his son
And held him for awhile
But then the boy asked to forgive
Which caused his dad to smile.

"My son, I do forgive you now
Because you've seen the light.
You need to know I love you so
And proud your heart wants right."

"I know you'll go apologize
And want to make amends
You'll do that since that is the place
Where healing all begins."

The boy replied, "Dad you're like God -
Who loved His Son so much
Who called to Him while on the cross
While longing for His touch."

"I hurt for you and long for you
I know what you have done -
I have forgiven every sin
Now come back home my son!"

Car Problems

I was sitting there in traffic with my windows all rolled up
And was tapping to the music drinking java from my cup;
I was comfy with my coffee sitting mellow in my seat
And my toes were getting thawed out from the blast of blowing heat.

There was ice on all my windows and more ice around the door
That I should have chipped and chiseled and I should have scraped off more;
Then as traffic started moving I drove 'round a traffic ring
While I sat there sipping Starbucks to the sounds of Seal and Sting.

When I turned the dial to country to the sound of Twitty's twang
It was then my comfort level would be altered with a bang;
All at once I felt a rumble that I hadn't felt before
And my car began to jostle spilling coffee on the floor.

I pulled over to the shoulder as my tires slid in a rut
Then I tried to lift the handle but the door was frozen shut.
I slid over to the right door and I also tried the latch
But then finding it was frozen too I kicked to free the catch.

I got out to see what happened and I saw I had a flat
So I scrambled in my car trunk for the stuff to handle that;
I pulled out a filthy blanket and my jack and cable pair
But the spare tire in the bottom was all worn and had no air.

I pulled out a red bandana and I waved it round my head
And I started saying loudly that I wish I'd stayed in bed;
I knew standing by the road side with a temperature of three
Was no way a situation that brought longer life to me.

[CAR PROBLEMS]

With my grounded car in frigid air I waved my rag and stood
And I knew that God would save me, as he promised me he would;
I was praying to my master and heard someone give a shout
It was Eddy, my big brother, who had stopped to help me out.

He then helped me fix my tire and a new spare behind the seat
Ed has always been so good to me with fellowship so sweet;
So now I have no problem with my car because I'm ready
But if I do, I'll ask God to be sending brother Eddy.

The Land Of Pleasant Dreams

To the land of Pleasant Dreams
Through a crystalline sea at night;
Children sail in ships of gold
Which the fairies guide by moonlight.

I have seen this magic land
Where the lollypop bush is grown;
In this land are gum drop trees
And large candy cane fields are known.

There big clouds of fluffy white
Start to magically change in shape;
They may look like teddy bears
Or transform to look like an ape.

There's a tree of chocolate there
That holds chocolate balls so round;
And inside of every sphere
There a caramel egg is found.

And there on top of a hill
The sweet taffy trees you will see;
And down in a pond below
There's the gummy fish swimming free.

In the land of Pleasant Dreams
Guardian angels will come to stay;
While they watch each child in sight
As they eat and then run and play.

[THE LAND OF PLEASANT DREAMS]

There's great joy and laughter there
With no worry of sadness meet;
With a breeze from angel wings
And a puppy dog at your feet.

Lay on the ground and you'll hear
A brook's happily flowing sigh;
The sounds are so soft and sweet
Like a kitty cat prancing by.

All are glad and feel at home
No one hurting or feeling blue;
There is beauty in every place
And the feeling of love is true.

In the land of Pleasant Dreams
Each child eagerly comes to play;
But soon they will sail back home
And rise meeting a brand new day.

What My Bible Means To Me

Worn and tattered as can be
Is the Bible given me
Many pages in God's word
Marked or torn or scored or blurred
Notes which show a favorite verse
Giving hope when things seem worse
Stains from tears through anguished prayer
Water marks are everywhere.

"Memorize" a note throughout
For great truths to know and spout
Many pages creased with wear
From my constant reading there.
Numerous verse I've underlined
Aiding me to easily find
As I read it every day
Something fresh I hear God say.

Meditate I love to do
Letting God teach something new
Sometimes God will call to me,
"Stop those things done selfishly"
Other times I hear his plea,
"Tell the world of Calvary"
It's alive and active still
Pointing out the Father's will.

It reads thoughts and heart and more
Cutting to the very core
Precious word of God has worth
Valued more than all the earth
If you want the keys of life
Live God's word the holy knife
Greater thing there's none to do but
Let the word of God in you.

Cleaning The Bathroom

I cleaned up the tub
Put sparkle on tiles
I scoured the floor
With joy and some smiles.

I placed in the dish
A new cake of soap
I Windexed the windows
Hung freshener by rope.

The toilet was cleaned
With cleanser and brush
It glistened and shimmered
With a flip and a flush.

You hear a slight squeak
Running fingers on rim
Smelled lemony fresh
Transformed bright from dim.

Just trying to please
To make life more merry
I like a bath cheerful
With no hint of scary.

Ring The Bell

As you lie there in your bed
May angels guard you tight;
Settle back and rest your head
Until the morning light.

God is lying next to you
So hold his loving arms;
Let him calm your troubles too
And quiet all alarms.

Singing you a lullaby
He helps you fall asleep;
Dreams begin with half a sigh
You slumber long and deep.

You're next to a Christmas tree
The pine smell's in the air;
You are with your family
Exchanging presents there.

Gazing at the gifts, you smile
Because they say "From God."
You receive one from the pile
The shape seems rather odd.

You unwrap a golden bell
And while you do you hum;
It has words on it as well,
"Just ring it and He'll come."

Suddenly it hits you fast
While staring at the gold;
Blinded by a brilliant blast.
An angel shouts, "Behold!"

[RING THE BELL]

"Do not let the sun go down
Before you ring the bell.
Shout to everyone in town
A 'Christ is Coming' yell!"

Then you start to run about
And yell, "Christ comes tonight!
Listen up and hear me shout -
Here comes the Son of Light!"

"It is not for me to say,"
Some shout, "God only knows.
It's His secret locked away -
That's what the Bible shows."

You acknowledge and agree,
"You're right as rain," You say.
"But it's best to be ready
Than lost and led astray."

You remind them why we're here -
To ring the gospel out;
And in Christ we should not fear
To share what love's about.

Watching sun begin to set
You start to ring the bell;
Seeing light get brighter yet
You shed your earthly shell.

God then greets you with a smile -
As you come face to face;
Then He hugs you for awhile
With one long warm embrace.

You wake up and start to pray,
"Dear Lord please let me ring
And share the news of Christ today
For You Almighty King!"

My Kind Sweet Sister

The greatest thing about my sis is she is kind at heart
She always looks for ways to serve and loves you from the start;
Whenever there's a hurt or pain she rushes in to mend
And doesn't stop her caring 'til the pain comes to an end.

Remembering back to long ago to memories that we made
Sis helped sell drinks and cookies at our stand of lemonade;
When customers had drank their cup and wanted to have more
Sis quickly took the pitcher up and started in to pour.

And then there was a time on bikes we pedaled from a hill
I flew down quick and slid on leaves and took a nasty spill;
My sister came to my aid quick and pulled me to my feet
And helped me get all dusted off and back onto my seat.

The mealtimes were another way that sis showed being kind
She offered food she liked to me and didn't really mind;
When there was only one slice left of Mom's brown sugar pie
My sister gave it up to me and smiled with gentle sigh.

One day I came home crying with a painful broken arm
My sister sat there close to me and calmed me with her charm;
She told me that I'd be alright and help was on the way
And when I came back with a cast she brought a game to play.

As years have passed she married with some children of her own
And gave them by example sweet kindness she's always shown;
She never stops her loving ways and gives 'til joy's restored
And keeps on serving those in need just like our heavenly Lord.

The Spot

In our house it was so peaceful and so quiet just last week
That's until we got the sofa which was bought at Jay's Antique;
It was Mom who planned the perfect place to put the sofa chair
And she had it situated in the den with utmost care.

We as children were permitted to sit lightly on the seat
But were never to bring candy to that place for us to eat;
We were also warned of spankings if we let a soda spill
On the surface of the cushion that was owned by a Churchill.

I did not know the addition would cause such a family feud
That's until my dear sweet mother found her chair with stains of food;
We could hear the rafters lifting as she raised her voice at us
And we ran to see what happened and to fess up or discuss.

There I stood and saw some mustard in the middle of the seat
That had come from someone's hotdog since a piece was at its feet;
Then our mother asked the question that we children hate to hear,
"Who has done this? Tell me quickly or you'll both not see next year."

I knew I was not the culprit and spoke up and said "Not I."
And when sister said the same thing that's when Mom could sense a lie;
She began to ask us questions as to what we'd had for lunch
And I said that I had hotdogs and my sis had Captain Crunch.

As she grew more irritated and she asked me where I sat
I just pointed to the kitchen at the table with the mat;
Then Mom asked me to please show her where I set up all my food
And I showed her in the kitchen without any sign of rude.

[THE SPOT]

Then our dog came in the kitchen with some mustard on its snout
And when Mother saw the mustard she then finally worked it out;
For our dog had somehow grabbed a snack and went to have a treat
On the only chair that Mom had warned no living soul shall eat.

I then helped Mom clean the cushion and it wasn't long at all
When the Churchill chair was right again and looked original;
So be careful in your family when you have a brand new chair
Not to get one you can't sit on and to have one not so rare.

Be Steadfast

Do not let go of the truths you know
Stand firm your ground to the end,
Just hold on tight, be a guiding light
And don't give up hope to the wind.

Through stress and strife in the storms of life
Just pray and stay close to God;
Then you'll prevail as you walk the trail
Where great men of faith there have trod.

So stand up tall to the Spirit's call
Be strong and brave, never bend;
Then you will see the great victory
Which the steadfast find at the end.

You must not fear since your God is near
The things that tear down a man;
For you will win every trial you're in
If you trust and cling to His plan.

There'll be a day you could walk away
When tempted to quit the fight;
But stay on pace, and you'll win the race
And receive a crown in His sight.

So stand up tall to the Spirit's call
Be strong and brave, never bend;
Then you will see the great victory
Which the steadfast find at the end

Remember Christ

Since storms will come and winds will blow
Since people die and conflicts grow
Since plans will fail and leaves turn brown
And friends will sometimes let you down
Remember who gives life and death
And loved us with his dying breath.

Since stocks will crash and chairmen lie
Since cancer kills and crime's too high
Since greed lives on and gang wars kill
And marriages are failing still
Remember Christ with insults hurled
Who hung with thieves to save the world.

Since children starve and mothers grieve
Since soldiers hurt and teens conceive
Since some will cheat and some don't care
And wars leave scars that all must bear
Remember Christ whose blood was shed
Who came to save us from the dead.

So don't give up and don't give in
Remember Christ who cleansed our sin
This world's a sick and wretched place
So share God's love and show God's grace
Keep loving and forget the past
Since those in Christ are free at last.

Whatever You Do To Haiti

Strike a nail for Haiti
Build a wall of hope
The wells must have clean water
And baths with brush and soap.

Clear the roads and walkways
Sweep the floors with joy
The food and clothes give quickly
To every girl and a boy.

Don't forget
Don't neglect
Don't turn your face and flee
"Whatever you do to them," he said,
"You do so also to me."

Lay another shingle
Hands of love to lend
The roofs are torn to pieces
From hurricane's high wind

Medicine and band aids
Needed every day
The mud and dirt are everywhere
Where children run and play.

Don't forget
Don't neglect
Don't turn your face and flee
"Whatever you do to them," he said,
"You do so also to me."

[WHATEVER YOU DO TO HAITI]

Some have lost their love ones
From floods by heavy rain.
Others need a shoulder
To cry on from the pain

All these folks need Jesus
The sick ones and the small
So please now turn your heart on and
Be Jesus to them all.

Don't forget
Don't neglect
Don't turn your face and flee
"Whatever you do to them," he said,
"You do so also to me."

Thank You For The Christmas Lights

Thank you for the lights you share
At Christmas time each year;
Thank you for the joy you bring
To others far and near.

Thank you for the strings of lights
That flash to melodies;
Thank you for the colors bright
On all your stringed up trees.

Thank you for the Santa Claus
Around your fireplace;
Thank you for the choo choo train
That circles in its place.

Thank you for the penguins that
Sit in a coaster seat;
Thank you for the airplane which
Has movement as a treat.

Thank you for the 'go-round too
Which adds a touch of class;
And all the little blinking
Of lights lined in the grass.

Joy is seen in every age
Kids spirits do you lift;
As a neighbor near to you
I thank you for your gift.

New Home Welcome

Welcome to your new home
I hope you settle fast
Unpacking of the boxes
The mayhem will not last.

The plates get put on shelf tops
The glasses put away
The silver placed in cabinets
And the napkins on the tray.

The beds have new positions
With a different morning view
The walls are freshly painted
And the carpet smells brand new.

The television's hooked up
With the sofa 'gainst the wall
And hifi speakers placed so
you hear music from the hall.

The table looks so pretty
With matching bowls and dishes
Your house is looking lovely
As I send these best of wishes.

God bless your home forever
As you share his gracious love
May peace and joy be with you
As he looks down from above.

Compared To God

The flash of time we call our lives
Is just a wink to God
And all man's words to Him can be
Summed up with just a nod.

The light from all the stars combined
Don't shine like His own face
And what He sees is far beyond
What we have glimpsed in space.

The mighty storms and hurricanes
That stir up in the sky
Are just the noise and breath He makes
When He lets out a sigh.

And all the treasures and the wealth
That we could have on earth
Are nothing more than dross to God
Compared to what He's worth.

No wisdom can surpass our God's
Nor His philosophy
The universe He holds is small
Matched to His majesty.

God is so great and we're so small
It's wise to fear His name
For if we let God in our lives
We'll never be the same.

When A Child Leaves Home

We let go a child when they've reached the age
To spread their own wings and to earn their own wage
Although it is hard we must let them go
To reach for their dreams and not hinder them so.

We've done all we can if we steer them straight
To do what is right and learn patience to wait
For times to give service that meets a need
No matter if noticed they've done their good deed.

When dangers and troubles have come their way
We want to act quickly to help them and pray
But let us remember that through their trial
They'll grow more mature if we linger awhile.

And when they have victories, and they will too
We'll praise their resolve and for sticking it through
Then celebrate with them for what they've done
And share in their triumph as daughter and son.

As parents we all need to learn to trust
That God will take care of them as he does us
For we once left home with a heavy heart
And had our own parents who let us depart.

Remember the lesson that God has taught
Who watched as his son left his heavenly spot
And let him hang dying till all was done
So we all could share in his victory won.

The Dog Head Cookies

Some children found a dog head skull
While walking in the wood
And brought it home and hosed it off
And cleaned it best they could.

They took a shiny cookie pan
And cleared the oven door
And placed the dog head skull on it
To cook and clean some more.

The children had a plan to bring
The skull to school for show
But wanted first to kill the germs
By cooking it on low.

Then soon a smell filled up the room
And skull was thrown outside
The pan was thrown into the trash
And fans were open wide.

Much later on that afternoon
Someone pulled pan from trash
And placed it in the sink to clean
While leaving in a dash.

Then dad came home and saw the pan
And thought how good it'd be
To use the pan for cooking his
Own cookie recipe.

The smells of cooking chocolate chips
Soon filled up all the place
While cookies were all scraped off from
The pan by saving grace.

[THE DOG HEAD COOKIES]

Then friend of dad's came in and smelled
Some cookies near the sink
Who grabbed them up and ate them all
And then went for a drink.

The truth came out much later on
And friend's still friends with dad
But friend still thinks the crumbs he ate
Were best he's ever had.

One Special Night

As some shepherds watched their sheep
Angels came with news to keep
In a stable Christ will sleep
Now in Bethlehem, he's here.

While they watched, the shepherds froze
Terrified down to their toes
Seeing how a cherub glows
The angel said, "Do not fear."

In the stillness of that night
There a wondrous star so bright
Beamed to be a guiding light
Showed the way to the new king.

Gold or velvet none for bed
Just a trough to lay his head
In a place where cattle fed
That's the spot where angels sing.

Shepherds came to see the child
While he lay there meek and mild
Among creatures that were wild
And gave praise to God above.

In that precious holy night
God gave first the gift of light
To a world with sinful blight
Reaching out with perfect love.

Please Give Me A Pen

I went to her room at a quarter past four
Shook gently the handle and knocked on her door.
I called out my name and asked, "Please let me in,"
And waited there hoping to borrow a pen.
A voice from inside shouted, "Please go away,
I'm doing my homework. I've had a tough day."
I told her I did not intend to intrude
But needed a pen to write down lists of food.
With that she responded, "I'll get one, please wait,"
And then came the silent delay that I hate.

I stared at her door with the signs hanging there
Which read, "Do Not Enter," "Stay Out" and "Beware."
Amused I stood thinking of previous times
My child let me in to read old nursery rhymes.
She always would let me come into her space
For games and tea parties and snacks after grace.

I stood there awhile with my thoughts of the past
But finally I said, "Please, I need a pen fast."
At that I heard movement and words, "Can't you wait?"
And then through the door came a black Papermate.
My daughter then spoke up, "I'm sorry dear Dad.
I've tests to prepare for so please don't be mad."
And as her door closed we pretended we kissed
Then back in the kitchen I wrote up my list.

At The Trumpet Call

With the trumpet call of God
Heaven's gates will open wide
There will stand the Son of man
With the angels at his side

We will see him there above
In His majesty so bright
There His radiant hosts will shine
In a beam of brilliant light.

Are you ready for his call
If He comes back here tonight?
Do you want to risk it all
By not oiling up your light?

To prepare for Him today
Trust God's word in all you read
And in Christ give self away
For no day is guaranteed.

All whose names are written in
God's great scroll; The book of Life
Will at once be lifted up
From this world of sin and strife.

Those who still are left behind
Will then fall down on their knees
And will have to give account
For their acts and sinful deeds.

[AT THE TRUMPET CALL]

Are you ready for the blast
If He comes back here today?
Have you turned to Christ at last
Or do you know what you'll say?

It is now all up to you
How you plan for Christ's return.
You can choose to live anew -
Or is death not your concern?

Hello and Goodbye

"Hello there" and "howdy" and "how do you do?"
"What you been up to" and "what's up with you?"
"Welcome" and "morning" and "hi" and "good day."
These are some greetings we all love to say.

All courtesy, kindness and caring are good
Along with respect which shows praise as we should;
But when we meet others do we stay awhile
And share a kind word to bring hope and a smile?

"Bye now" and "see you" and "I've got to run"
"Time to get going" and "Well, it's been fun."
"Good night" and "goodbye" and "I've got to go."
These are some parting words we say and know.

We tell them these words as we're walking out then
Assuming we'll see them and greet them again;
But may I suggest as we leave and depart -
We give them a blessing that comes from the heart.

A Headache

A headache is an awful feeling
As it makes you hit the ceiling
From the growing pain pulsation
And the throbbing main sensation.
It can come at any hour
And will take away your power
Sending shockwaves through your senses
Tearing down all known defenses.
When your head starts pounding badly
You will take some aspirin gladly
Which should ease the blood constriction
And bring calm to your affliction.
As you wait and while you simmer
Lights turned off help make it dimmer
But sometimes in utter silence
You'll give way to sudden violence
As your eyes are slightly squinting
Stabbing pain is unrelenting.
Which will send your stomach wheeling
As you stand there, stooping, reeling.
That's the time you start confessing
And thank God for every blessing
Though in time it will subside
It teaches you to give up pride.
When it's through you'll feel much better
As it seems to break the fetter
Of all the rage inside your head –
But just in case, go lie in bed.

Through The Twilight

It's now twilight time oh sweet child of mine,
With sun going down in the sky;
The colors have spread up over your head
While clouds of light crimson pass by.
A sole whippoorwill sings out a song 'til
The last sunlight beam fades away;
And then comes the night with beacons of light
From stars in the great milky way.

The moon starts to rise from low in the skies -
It shines with proportions immense;
Large craters that show form a face all a glow
And beams light around so intense.
Just then comes a breeze that runs through the trees
Which sway like the seas on a plain;
And then you inhale a jasmine scent trail
That's outside your raised windowpane.

So lie now in bed my young sleepy head
Let's pray to the Lord - close your eyes;
I'll ask God above to show you His love
And to help you grow stronger and wise.
I pray you will shine like a star as a sign
That you serve only Christ 'til you die;
My hope is you'll share, and through twilight care
So you'll go to the Son in the sky.

It's Not Because

It's not because of how you serve
That blesses every saint
Nor is it by the notes you write
In pencil, pen or paint.

It's not because of how you love
That aids in hospice care
Although you hope to touch the lives
Of ones you visit there.

It's not because of what you give
That helps the sick and poor
Nor is it all the times you pray
That quickens healing more.

It's not because of what you say
That brings one to the light
Nor is it when you share the truth
That one will do what's right.

It's also not at all because
You touch some lives abroad
By preaching in their native tongue
That turns their lives to God.

But it's because of God who gives
Each blessing to uplift
And uses us to spread His love
Which is His perfect gift.

Don't Let Pride Get In The Way

What is it that's keeping us
From bowing to God in prayer?
When we have troubles in our lives
We try hard not to share.

Why is it so difficult
To stop and ask advice?
When we see all the signs to stop
We go and don't think twice.

Why is it that every time
We get but don't thank God?
The things we have are not enough;
They're getting old or flawed.

Don't let pride get in the way
Don't lie and say it's fine.
Put self to death and follow God
Serve others and you'll shine.

Who do we give credit to
When others praise our acts?
We tend to boast and cheer ourselves
By patting our own backs.

Which love do we understand
Will thrive on selfishness?
Go look around and soon we'll find
No love can live with this.

[DON'T LET PRIDE GET IN THE WAY]

When do we say, "Thank you Lord,
For all that you have done;
For giving us eternal life
By giving us your son?"

Don't let pride get in the way
Don't lie and say it's fine.
Put self to death and follow God
Love others and you'll shine.

It's God Who Sees Everything

It's God who sees what we cannot and knows ahead of time
The heights we'll reach if we'll seek Him and dare to make the climb;
We can not grasp the power of God or his redeeming grace
Which he pours out to everyone who longs for his embrace.

We tend to criticize and judge by raising up the bar
And note the flaws of everyone while labeling who they are;
But God sees far beyond all that and sees what we can be
When we seek Christ and trust His word and follow faithfully.

God sees the good in each of us before we even start
And sees the hurts and hang ups too from deep inside our heart;
We cannot hide a thing from God, he sees us everywhere
He sees our sins and sees our joys and sees our every care.

It's God who sees what we will see and sees what we should not
He sees and knows what's best for us and sees what tempts a lot;
It's we who need to focus on the things God sees as right
And learn to see with Godly eyes to serve Him day and night.

We can not see the spans of time which God can blink away
Nor see a far out universe which God sees every day;
But we have eyes He's given us to see, and look and stare
So use your eyes to praise His name and serve Him everywhere.

Some Good Questions

What shall we say?
Why do we live?
How do we serve?
When do we give?

These are some questions
We ask God each day
When we bow down
And silently pray.

Who shall we tell?
How do we share?
When should we speak?
Why do we care?

Ask God for answers
If ever in doubt
Let him remind us
What love's all about.

Who died for us?
Who rose again?
Who gave us life?
Who cleansed our sin?

This is the message
We're all called to give
Share Christ with others
As long as we live.

Why You Are So Beautiful

Holding candles to your beauty
There's no one that has that duty
Just like rocks that have no luster
Placed next to a diamond cluster
They may look like model women
But have hearts like sour lemon
You're the one whose heart is pure
And it's your charm that will endure.

Passing time you shine more brightly
As you sprinkle kindness lightly
On the hurting and the lonely
Thinking not of self but only
Trying to encourage others
Serving strangers, sisters, brothers
You're the one whose love is true
And you have God alive in you.

You're more prized than any ruby
Just like Christ I see you to be
Giving others joy and blessing
With the love of God confessing
Only God receives the credit
And not you but Christ who said it
The pure heart will see God's face
And that's why you excel in grace.

These Twenty-Seven Years

I pray and thank my Father
For a wife so heavenly
I can't help think how blessed
I am to have you next to me;
We've had our times of gladness
And our share of grief and tears
I know our love is deeper now
These twenty-seven years.

I still remember of the day
You wore that dress of red
I still recall you baking me
My first banana bread;
I loved the dates we had at school
And fun we had with peers
I've always loved to hold your hand
These twenty-seven years.

You have a way of showing love
With kindness in your heart
That warms and heals the sad and sick -
You're gifted in that art;
You're full of wisdom and of wit
As everybody cheers
I love your humor best of all
These twenty-seven years.

Your hair is dark and radiant
Your hands are soft but strong
Your smile is so contagious
I could watch it all day long;
Your eyes and nose are beautiful -
I love to touch your ears
But when we kiss I always melt
These twenty-seven years.

If Jesus Came Back Here Tonight

If Jesus came back here tonight
Would you be glad He came?
Would you rejoice in seeing Him
Or would you feel the shame?

If you heard trumpets overhead
And saw our Lord appear -
Would you go to your home above
Or stay on earth in fear?

Think back to all the plans you've made
Would they give God the praise?
Or would your plans bring folks to Him
In all the coming days?

If Jesus came would he know you
For following God's will?
Or would He say, "Depart from me,
I never knew you still"?

If Christ came back to earth tonight
Would those you know arise?
Would they have Christ as their Lord too
And float up to the skies?

So is your hope in Jesus Christ?
And have you found the light?
Do you await eternal life
If Jesus came tonight?

The Sweet Lullaby

The sails of the dream ship are silken and spread,
While sweet gentle breezes blow flags overhead.
The sea gleams by moonlight and dark starry sky;
The name of the dream ship is "Sweet Lullaby."

The ship's built by fairies and magic it seems,
And sails to Port Slumber with all children's dreams.
When all of the child dreams have sailed over there,
Each child will rise soundly without any care.

The sandman is captain who pilots the ship,
And precious the cargo that makes every trip.
What a wonderful ship, the Sweet Lullaby,
Which sails by the moon in a dark starry sky.

As the ship is at sea, the angels descend;
They watch and they guard all the dreams without end.
The angels keep dream counts as each has a number;
Then angels will count them again at Port Slumber.

The sand of the sandman makes dreams settle down;
When dreams are stirred up and are tossed all aroun'.
The sandman has fairies as helpers on board;
Who watch the chests closely where all the sand's stored.

Then the dreams come to port through the darkest of night;
And each child wakes in peace by the bright morning light.
For it's due to a ship, the Sweet Lullaby,
Which sails by the moon in a dark starry sky.

I'm Proud Of You Son

You're now on your own
You make your own bed
You've suddenly grown
New thoughts fill your head.

It's time to do right
Keep up with your studies
Late homework at night
Great times with your buddies.

I'm proud of you son.

Seek help when in need
Your teachers are great
Apply what you read
Don't stay up too late.

Please find a temp job
To help pay for books
Eat corn on the cob
Stay thin with good looks.

I'm proud of you son.

The chapel is great
Be prompt to your seat
In class don't be late
Find clubs and compete.

But most of all grow
In your love for God
Show your friends you know
Where eagles have trod.

I'm proud of you son.

The Fall Of The Mighty Kong

The mighty Kong was hanging there
Just dangling from a spire
While watching all the fighter jets
Fly round him even higher.
He saw a blimp come passing by
And jumped on top of it
Which caused the blimp to sink and strike
The spires of Saint Patrick.
The impact caused the blimp to pop
Which sent King Kong in space
And as he flew the world could see
The anguish on his face.
King Kong at last did come to earth
And landed in the bay
And when he did a voice replied.
"Thank you, You made my day!"
King Kong then saw Godzilla there
Emerging into view
And showed him every courtesy
As if a friend he knew.
"Please let me help you up my friend
And left me dry you off."
With that he blew hot air on Kong
And dried his wooly cloth.
The King of Kong replied and said,
"Why thank you very much.
I know a place where we can eat
White shark and whale and such."
So the two friends swam out to sea
Fading into sunset
Now best of friends they're glad the day
That Kong fell and they met.

My Mother's Love

The times have changed and things are not
The same as they once were
But you have been a constant source
Of love my dear mother;
Though wars go on as conflicts rise
Way out of our control
You share a type of peaceful love
That comforts all my soul.

I love the way you call on me
And ask me how's my day
You seem to know ahead of time
When trials have come my way;
Like when I'm sick or down and out
With challenges in view
I get a letter in the mail
With loving words from you.

You find and give me gifts of love
That bring me constant joy
You share great words of wisdom too
To bless your little boy;
I see your love in cooking food
When I sit down to eat
You'll make me custard lemon cakes
Or a brown sugar treat.

I see how much you love the birds
That perch up in your tree
And love to search our family roots
To find more history;
I know you love to hear God's word
Or read a Christian book
You treasure all the family times
And love the photo book.

[MY MOTHER'S LOVE]

Your love is just so wonderful
And plain for all to see
I hope and pray I share such love
As you have shown to me;
I thank you for a mother's love
For all the joy you bring
I know your love is sent from God
And makes the angels sing.

A Message By The Sea

She gazed upon the moonlit sky
While on a promenade
And stood on periwinkle shells
Next to the sea with God.

"Dear Lord," she asked, "What must I do
To glorify your name?
For William has deserted me
And brought me grief and shame."

She stood in silence by the shore
With hope for God's reply
And prayed a prayer for comfort then
As she began to cry.

A zephyr whisked her hair and then
An angel touched her tears
It spoke with loving tenderness
And took away her fears.

"Don't let your heart be troubled now,
And dry your tears away.
God has prepared a place for you,
So Trust Him every day."

The angel left with these few words
As she bent knees to bow.
"I thank you Lord for showing me
To trust you here and now."

With many words she praised the Lord
In quiet on the shore
Then left with hope while looking toward
The place God has in store.

Turn The Radio Off!

I left the radio on loud next to the room of Jack
The music sounded staticy with treble out of whack;
It wasn't long before I heard my brother shouting mad,
"Please hurry turn the radio off! It hurts my ears so bad!"

I quickly jumped up to my feet and ran across the room
And stumbled on a pair of shoes and tripped over a broom;
And heard him yell as I got up with all the strength he had,
"Please hurry turn the radio off! It hurt's my ears so bad!"

I went and hit the mute control and went to make a snack
And found a pot for cooking on top of the cooking rack;
As I got it the pots fell down and made an awful noise
And then I heard my brother say, "Keep quiet in there boys!"

I made some soup and sandwiches and offered some to Jack
He thanked me but he turned it down since sleep is what he lacked;
I went back to the kitchen and tripped over kitty's dish
Then heard my brother yelling back, "Silence is all I wish!"

I finished cleaning up the pans and went back toward my room
And told my brother as I went, "I'm sorry for the boom."
Then Jack told me it was alright but he was trying to sleep
So he could work the late night shift, so not another peep.

I told him that I'd let him sleep and that just made him smile
I tip toed back into my room and sat to read awhile;
But then I sat on my remote destroying the peace I had
"Please hurry turn the radio off! It hurts my ears so bad!"

For All You Do For Scouts

You fold and hang up all your scout clothes,
And put up your tarp and your bags;
You wash off your boots and your tent stakes,
And wipe down your tent with some rags.

It was a great hike with your scout troop,
And know it was worth all the pain;
You watched boys who started out grumbling
Become men while cheering the rain.

You helped and encouraged a young scout
Who struggled with gear and his mood;
Then later in camp he was cheerful
While in his patrol cooking food.

You saw leadership there in action
While crossing a deep flowing stream;
When older scouts helped with the younger,
You praised all their work as a team

The skills that you saw on the scout trip
With fears overcome by your lead,
Will stick with these boys through the ages,
And help them as men to succeed.

So thank you for being a mentor,
And thank you for being a friend;
For showing boys how to be leaders
Which changes our world in the end.

What Is My Purpose Here?

What really is my purpose here?
And how come I was born?
Throughout each day and every year
I'm empty and forlorn.
I find I'm active in myself,
While I completely live for self;
I love to praise and give myself
A toot and blow my horn.

I know there's something I've left out
Because I'm not complete.
I need that thing without a doubt
So I can rest my feet.
I'm tired of the race each day,
While picking up the pace each day,
And keeping a straight face each day;
My troubles have me beat.

I think it's time to bring Christ in
And let him rule my life
He just might clean my slate of sin
And rid me of my strife.
I have a lot of mess inside
I need to just confess, not hide
To ease the pain and stressful tide
That stabs me like a knife.

I've read the scriptures and obeyed
The gospel, now I'm free!
I live to serve now unafraid
Where after death I'll be.
I have the Spirit, a heavenly dove
Which came down from the Lord above
Because of one with perfect love
Who died upon a tree.

The Time I Spend

The time I spend to read God's word
With children in their bed
Is wiser spent than reading books
On how to get ahead.
The time I spend to pray aloud
For needs of hurting folk
Is wiser spent than praying soft
For ways to not go broke.
The time I have is not my own
God's numbered all my days
The wisest thing I'll ever do
Is serve and give Him praise.

The time I spend to help unload
When someone's moving in
Is wiser spent than working out
Through training discipline.
The time I spend with family
Even when times are tough
Is wiser spent than business trips
With all its corporate stuff.
I know God brings eternal joy
To those who love and give
So I will spend my time on earth
To serve God well and live.

A Christian Prayer

In Christ we have the same name
In Christ we're family
In Christ we have all riches
In Christ we're royalty.
The strength comes from his Spirit
The power is there as well
I pray that you will plug in him
And in your hearts he'll dwell.

Christ's love does not have reason
Christ's love does not have rhyme
Christ's love costs not a penny
Christ's love costs all your time
There is no way to grasp it
It blows the mind it's true
How wide and long and high and deep
The love Christ has for you.

Get rooted in the King's Son
Get established in his love
Get filled up by his Spirit
Get riches from above
Share Christ with others always
Who cleanses every sin
Then give God all the glory and praise
Forever and amen.

Fireworks With The Family

Firecrackers blasting loudly
Making folks jump to their feet;
Alex lights a rocket proudly
Then backs off and takes a seat.
Everyone then hears a banging
Tracking its launch with their eyes
Ears recover from the clanging
As the colors fill the skies.

Ethan fires a Roman Candle -
Crackling lights go everywhere
Sparklers are not hard to handle;
Maggie waves them in the air.
Then Amanda lights "The Killer"
As it hisses on the ground;
Boys jump back to watch a thriller
From the lights and from the sound.

Then the ground begins a'shaking
As the mortar shells explode;
Sister fears her crystal's breaking
From the noise near her abode.
Flowering colors fill the twilight
Shimmering light in all degrees;
Everyone stares at the bright light
As it goes over the trees.

Then there is applause and laughter
Begging comes to shoot some more;
After that a few right after
Are shot up and make a roar.
Then we give thanks for good weather
And the time to eat and play
Thanking God we're here together
And our independence day.

From Pieces of Wood

Pieces of wood in the artisan's hands
With care they're studied and viewed;
Looking them over 'til he understands
How they'll be fitted and glued.

With great devotion he takes on the chore
Carving out each from a mold;
Skilled hands in motion chips fall to the floor
Transforming wood into gold.

After he's varnished he puts down the brush
The instrument dries in the sun;
Finishing touches are made with no rush
Tools are laid down. It is done.

Taking a bow he starts playing the strings
The gorgeous sound slowly ceases;
He starts to praise God while laughing and sings
It's God who makes masterpieces!

A Lifeless Heart

A lifeless heart does not a thing
Because it doesn't beat;
It isn't good for anything,
Like legs without their feet.

It has no love to give inside
To pour and touch again.
Its vessels are all filled with pride;
With chambers full of sin.

No tears are shed from sympathy.
No joy or hope is known;
The heart cannot feel empathy
Because it's cold as stone.

The useless organ will not give
To hurts and needs in sight;
From self-sickness it does not live
To serve and do what's right.

This selfish heart needs God's embrace
To start the pulse to pound;
With broken humble pleas for grace,
And knees down on the ground.

The only way to heal this heart
Is found in Christ who lives;
With sins washed clean as a jump-start,
Agape love it gives.

Symphonic Ecstasy

As horns from the orchestra silence,
   and stillness is felt in the air,
The bows of the strings move together,
   and play as if God were there.
A lush sound of celli infusing
   the theme that the violins play,
While each note that's played and suspended,
   takes everyone's breath away.

Then up from the glorious rapture,
   with tones that are all heaven sent;
The sound of the English Horn rises
   and pours out its dark lament.
What beauty is heard from an angel
   who sings in a lower key,
Through grains of the Grenadilla,
   with it's haunting melody.

But then in an instant there's fanfare,
   as trumpets and baritones soar;
The timpani joins with the tuba
   while all play the recap once more.
And when the last chord played has ended,
   and when all the echoes have died,
The walls and the ceiling start shaking,
   because the creator has cried.

When I See You

When I see you lie in bed
With little hands and curly head;
I stop to thank God for awhile
For blessing me with you, my child.
You are my babe for me to love -
I offer you to God above.

When I see you go to school
With lunch and books and measuring rule;
I stop to think how much you've grown
With hems let out and buttons sewn.
But still you are my babe to love -
I offer you to God above.

When I see you college bound
With car packed full and leaving town;
I hold my spouse and cry out loud
And hope dear child you'll make us proud.
You'll always be my babe to love -
I offer you to God above.

When I see you're mission sent,
I understand what Jesus meant;
To go in all the world to make
Disciples and thy self forsake.
So go and teach! Oh babe I love -
I offer you to God above.

When I see you at God's throne
As Jesus claims you as His own;
I'll run and leap and shout with glee
And hold you for eternity.
My babe, forever in Christ's love -
Who offered self to God above!

House Church With The Hixsons

The Hixson house church is getting ready
Nibbling in the kitchen, we can't wait
Jane's at the oven making spaghetti
George samples some food and says, "It's great."

Lee and Mary sit on a lover's chair
Paul comes in and takes off his old cap
Patty helps Jane put out the silverware
Dog Neo puts head on Maggie's lap.

Elizabeth brings some 'nana puddin'
Paul begins to creep to where it's at
Wayne just looks at Paul and says he shouldn'
'Cause if he eats too much, he'll get fat.

Vickie brings in fresh bread from the baker
Debbie H turns and gives a big, "Yeah!"
Gary then asks who'll be the prayer taker
Lee grabs up the pad and says he'll pray.

The prayer's said, then we share Bible verses
Mark and Helen come with drinks to sip
Gary shares God's blessings and His curses
While Alex eats some chips with his dip.

Some take communion before the dinner
Some go to the kitchen to take part
Meeting at the Hixson's is a winner, 'cause
Jesus is at the center of each heart.

The poems in this book were set in 10 point Century Schoolbook.

OTHER POETRY BY PAUL RAY

If you enjoyed

Scattered Glimpses
LEAVES OF POETRY

you may also like

Upwords
A FLIGHT OF POETRY
ISBN 978-0-578-03647-2
available online at lulu.com

www.ingramcontent.com/pod-product-compliance
Ingram Content Group UK Ltd.
Pitfield, Milton Keynes, MK11 3LW, UK
UKHW041228200426
11947UKWH00034B/441